*Atlantis, the Gods of Antiquity
and the Myth of the Dying God*

By
Manly P. Hall

ISBN: 978-1-63118-498-7

Esoteric Classics

Other Books in this Series and Related Titles

Freemasonry and the Egyptian Mysteries by C W Leadbeater (978-1-63118-456-7)

The Mysteries of Freemasonry & the Druids by M P Hall &c (978-1-63118-444-4)

Magical Essays and Instructions by Florence Farr (978-1-63118-418-5)

Arcane Formulas or Mental Alchemy by W W Atkinson (978-1-63118-459-8)

The Machinery of the Mind by Dion Fortune (978-1-63118-451-2)

The Hymn of Jesus by G. R. S. Mead (978-1-63118-492-5)

Buddhist Psalms by Shinran (978-1-63118-465-9)

Confessions of an English Opium-Eater by T De Quincey (978-1-63118-485-7)

Qabbalistic Teachings and the Tree of Life by M P Hall (978-1-63118-482-6)

Rosicrucian Rules, Secret Signs, Codes and Symbols by various (978-1-63118-488-8)

The Sepher Yetzirah and the Qabalah by M P Hall (978-1-63118-481-9)

Fortune-Telling with Dice by Astra Cielo (978-1-63118-466-6)

The Janeites, The Man Who Would Be King and Other Stories of Freemasonry by Rudyard Kipling (978-1-63118-480-2)

Crystal Vision Through Crystal Gazing by Achad (978-1-63118-455-0)

Psalms of Solomon by King Solomon (978-1-63118-439-0)

The Path of Light: A Manual of Maha-Yana Buddhism (978-1-63118-471-0)

The Book of the Watchers by Enoch (978-1-63118-416-1)

The Gospel of the Nativity of Mary by St. Matthew (978-1-63118-448-2)

A Collection of Fiction and Essays by Occult Writers on Supernatural, Metaphysical and Esoteric Subjects by various (978-1-63118-712-4)

The Leadbeater Reader: A Selection of Occult Essays (978-1-63118-483-3)

Audio versions are also available on Audible, Amazon and Apple

Table of Contents

INTRODUCTION

The word "esoteric" can be difficult to define. Esotericism in general can be seen less as a system of beliefs and more as a category, which encompasses numerous, different systems of beliefs. It's a bit of juxtaposition, since the word "esoteric" indicates something that few people know about, while the term itself broadly covers numerous philosophies, practices, areas of study and belief systems.

In a greater sense, Esotericism acts as a storehouse for secret knowledge, which is often considered ancient (by *tradition, if not by fact)*, passed down from generation to generation, in private. At various times in history, simply possessing the knowledge of some of these subjects, was considered illegal and a jailable offence, if discovered. This usually included such general topics as Alchemy, Pharmacology, Qabalah, Hermeticism, Occultism, Ceremonial Magic, Astrology, Divination, Rosicrucianism and so on. Collectively, these areas of study were often referred to as the esoteric sciences.

Sometimes, the outer garment of a subject isn't esoteric, while what is hidden beneath it, is. As an example, Freemasonry isn't necessarily esoteric by nature (at *least not anymore)*, but certain signs, passwords and handshakes given to the candidate during their initiation, are in fact, esoteric, in the sense that they are hidden from the general public.

Today, in the twenty-first century, such topics are readily available at bookstores across the country, and numerous mainsteam publishers offer beginners guides and coffee-table volumes on many of these subjects, intended for mass appeal. Books like *"The Secret"* have turned previously arcane topics into household knowledge. All that being the case, however, it isn't to say that there still aren't buried secrets to uncover, ancient wisdom being ignored and forgotten mysteries to be explored. In fact, it is often that we are only able to further our own studies by standing on the shoulders of these disappearing giants.

Lamp of Trismegistus is doing its part to help preserve humanity's esoteric history by making some of these classics available to those students who are seeking to unearth the knowledge of these ancient colossi.

So, be sure to check other titles from our *Esoteric Classics* series, as well as our *Occult Fiction, Theosophical Classics, Foundations of Freemasonry Series, Supernatural Fiction, Paranormal Research Series, Studies in Buddhism* and our *Christian Apocrypha Series*. You can also download the audio versions of most of these titles from Amazon, Apple or Audible, for learning on the go.

ATLANTIS
& THE GODS OF ANTIQUITY

Part I:
Descriptions of Atlantis

Atlantis is the subject of a short but important article appearing in the Annual Report of the Board of Regents of The Smithsonian Institution for the year ending June 30th, 1915. The author, M. Pierre Termier, a member of the Academy of Sciences and Director of Service of the Geologic Chart of France, in 1912 delivered a lecture on the Atlantean hypothesis before the Institut Océanographique; it is the translated notes of this remarkable lecture that are published in the Smithsonian report.

"After a long period of disdainful indifference," writes M. Termier, "observe how in the last few years science is returning to the study of Atlantis. How many naturalists, geologists, zoologists, or botanists are asking one another today whether Plato has not transmitted to us, with slight amplification, a page from the actual history of mankind. No affirmation is yet permissible; but it seems more and more evident that a vast region, continental or made up of great islands, has collapsed west of the Pillars of Hercules, otherwise called the Strait of Gibraltar, and that its collapse occurred in the not far distant past. In any event, the question of Atlantis is placed anew before men of science; and since I do not believe that it can ever be solved without the aid of oceanography, I have thought it natural to discuss it here, in this temple of maritime science, and to call to such a problem, long scorned but now being revived, the attention of oceanographers, as well as the attention of those who, though immersed in the tumult of cities, lend an ear to the distant murmur of the sea."

In his lecture M. Termier presents geologic, geographic, and zoologic data in substantiation of the Atlantis theory. Figuratively draining the entire bed of the Atlantic Ocean, he considers the inequalities of its basin and cites locations on a line from the Azores to Iceland where dredging has brought lava to the surface from a depth of 3,000 meters. The volcanic nature of the islands now existing in the Atlantic Ocean corroborates Plato's statement that the Atlantean continent was destroyed by volcanic cataclysms. M. Termier also advances the conclusions of a young French zoologist, M. Louis Germain, who admitted the existence of an Atlantic continent connected with the Iberian Peninsula and with Mauritania and prolonged toward the south so as to include some regions of desert climate. M. Termier concludes his lecture with a graphic picture of the engulfment of that continent.

The description of the Atlantean civilization given by Plato in the *Critias* may be summarized as follows. In the first ages the gods divided the earth among themselves, proportioning it according to their respective dignities. Each became the peculiar deity of his own allotment and established therein temples to himself, ordained a priestcraft, and instituted a system of sacrifice. To Poseidon was given the sea and the island continent of Atlantis. In the midst of the island was a mountain which was the dwelling place of three earth-born primitive human beings--Evenor; his wife, Leucipe; and their only daughter, Cleito. The maiden was very beautiful, and after the sudden death of her parents she was wooed by Poseidon, who begat by her five pairs of male children. Poseidon apportioned his continent among these ten, and Atlas, the eldest, he made overlord of the other nine. Poseidon further called the country *Atlantis* and the surrounding sea the *Atlantic* in honor of Atlas. Before the birth of his ten sons, Poseidon divided the continent and the coastwise sea into concentric zones of land and water, which were as perfect as though turned upon a lathe. Two zones of land and three of water surrounded the central island, which Poseidon caused to be irrigated with two springs of water--one warm and the other cold.

The descendants of Atlas continued as rulers of Atlantis, and with wise government and industry elevated the country to a position of surpassing dignity. The natural resources of Atlantis were apparently limitless. Precious metals were mined, wild animals domesticated, and perfumes distilled from its fragrant flowers. While enjoying the abundance natural to their semitropic location, the Atlanteans employed themselves also in the erection of palaces, temples, and docks. They bridged the zones of sea and later dug a deep canal to connect the outer ocean with the central island, where stood the palaces And temple of Poseidon, which excelled all other structures in magnificence. A network of bridges and canals was created by the Atlanteans to unite the various parts of their kingdom.

Plato then describes the white, black, and red stones which they quarried from beneath their continent and used in the construction of public buildings and docks. They circumscribed each of the land zones with a wall, the outer wall being covered with brass, the middle with tin, and the inner, which encompassed the citadel, with orichalch. The citadel, on the central island, contained the pal aces, temples, and other public buildings. In its center, surrounded by a wall of gold, was a sanctuary dedicated to Cleito and Poseidon. Here the first ten princes of the island were born and here each year their descendants brought offerings. Poseidon's own temple, its exterior entirely covered with silver and its pinnacles with gold, also stood within the citadel. The interior of the temple was of ivory, gold, silver, and orichalch, even to the pillars and floor. The temple contained a colossal statue of Poseidon standing in a chariot drawn by six winged horses, about him a hundred Nereids riding on dolphins. Arranged outside the building were golden statues of the first ten kings and their wives.

In the groves and gardens were hot and cold springs. There were numerous temples to various deities, places of exercise for men and for beasts, public baths, and a great race course for horses. At various vantage points on the zones were fortifications, and to the great harbor came vessels from every maritime nation. The zones were so thickly populated that the sound of human voices was ever in the air.

That part of Atlantis facing the sea was described as lofty and precipitous, but about the central city was a plain sheltered by mountains renowned for their size, number, and beauty. The plain yielded two crops each year,, in the winter being watered by rains and in the summer by immense irrigation canals, which were also used for transportation. The plain was divided into sections, and in time of war each section supplied its quota of fighting men and chariots.

THE SCHEME OF THE UNIVERSE ACCORDING TO THE GREEKS AND ROMANS.
From Cartari's *Imagini degli Dei degli Antichi.*[1]

---

[1] By ascending successively through the fiery sphere of Hades, the spheres of water, Earth, and air, and the heavens of the moon, the plane of Mercury is reached. Above Mercury are the planes of Venus, the sun, Mars, Jupiter, and Saturn, the latter containing the symbols of the Zodiacal constellations. Above the arch of the heavens (*Saturn*) is the dwelling Place of the different powers controlling the universe. The supreme council of the gods is composed of twelve deities--six male and six female--which correspond to the positive and negative signs of the zodiac. The six gods are Jupiter, Vulcan, Apollo, Mars, Neptune, and Mercury; the six goddesses are Juno, Ceres, Vesta, Minerva, Venus, and Diana. Jupiter rides his eagle as the symbol of his sovereignty over the world, and Juno is seated upon a peacock, the proper symbol of her haughtiness and glory.

13

The ten governments differed from each other in details concerning military requirements. Each of the kings of Atlantis had complete control over his own kingdom, but their mutual relationships were governed by a code engraved by the first ten kings on a column of orichalch standing in the temple of Poseidon. At alternate intervals of five and six years a pilgrimage was made to this temple that equal honor might be conferred upon both the odd and the even numbers. Here, with appropriate sacrifice, each king renewed his oath of loyalty upon the sacred inscription. Here also the kings donned azure robes and sat in judgment. At daybreak they wrote their sentences upon a golden tablet: and deposited them with their robes as memorials. The chief laws of the Atlantean kings were that they should not take up arms against each other and that they should come to the assistance of any of their number who was attacked. In matters of war and great moment the final decision was in the hands of the direct descendants of the family of Atlas. No king had the power of life and death over his kinsmen without the assent of a majority of the ten.

Plato concludes his description by declaring that it was this great empire which attacked the Hellenic states. This did not occur, however, until their power and glory had lured the Atlantean kings from the pathway of wisdom and virtue. Filled with false ambition, the rulers of Atlantis determined to conquer the entire world. Zeus, perceiving the wickedness of the Atlanteans, gathered the gods into his holy habitation and addressed them. Here Plato's narrative comes to an abrupt end, for the *Critias* was never finished. In the *Timæus* is a further description of Atlantis, supposedly given to Solon by an Egyptian priest and which concludes as follows:

"But afterwards there occurred violent earthquakes and floods; and in a single day and night of rain all your warlike men in a body sank into the earth, and the island of Atlantis in like manner disappeared, and was sunk beneath the sea. And that is the reason why the sea in those parts is impassable and impenetrable, because there is such a quantity of shallow mud in the way; and this was caused by the subsidence of the island."

In the introduction to his translation of the *Timæus*, Thomas Taylor quotes from a *History of Ethiopia* written by Marcellus, which contains the following reference to Atlantis: "For they relate that in their time there were seven islands in the Atlantic sea, sacred to Proserpine; and besides these, three others of an immense magnitude; one of which was sacred to Pluto, another to Ammon, and another, which is the middle of these, and is of a thousand stadia, to Neptune." Crantor, commenting upon Plato, asserted that the Egyptian priests declared the story of Atlantis to be written upon pillars which were still preserved circa 300 B.C.[2] Ignatius Donnelly, who gave the subject of Atlantis profound study, believed that horses were first domesticated by the Atlanteans, for which reason they have always been considered peculiarly sacred to Poseidon.[3]

---

[2] See *Beginnings or Glimpses of Vanished Civilizations*
[3] See *Atlantis*

From a careful consideration of Plato's description of Atlantis it is evident that the story should not be regarded as wholly historical but rather as both allegorical and historical. Origen, Porphyry, Proclus, Iamblichus, and Syrianus realized that the story concealed a profound philosophical mystery, but they disagreed as to the actual interpretation. Plato's Atlantis symbolizes the threefold nature of both the universe and the human body. The ten kings of Atlantis are the *tetractys*, or numbers, which are born as five pairs of opposites.[4] The numbers 1 to 10 rule every creature, and the numbers, in turn, are under the control of the Monad, or 1--the Eldest among them.

With the trident scepter of Poseidon these kings held sway over the inhabitants of the seven small and three great islands comprising Atlantis. Philosophically, the ten islands symbolize the triune powers of the Superior Deity and the seven regents who bow before His eternal throne. If Atlantis be considered as the archetypal sphere, then its immersion signifies the descent of rational, organized consciousness into the illusionary, impermanent realm of irrational, mortal ignorance. Both the sinking of Atlantis and the Biblical story of the "fall of man" signify spiritual involution--a prerequisite to conscious evolution.

Either the initiated Plato used the Atlantis allegory to achieve two widely different ends or else the accounts preserved by the Egyptian priests were tampered with to perpetuate the secret doctrine. This does not mean to imply

---

[4] Consult Theon of Smyrna for the Pythagorean doctrine of opposites.

that Atlantis is purely mythological, but it overcomes the most serious obstacle to acceptance of the Atlantis theory, namely, the fantastic accounts of its origin, size, appearance, and date of destruction--9600 B.C. In the midst of the central island of Atlantis was a lofty mountain which cast a shadow five thousand stadia in extent and whose summit touched the sphere of *æther*. This is the axle mountain of the world, sacred among many races and symbolic of the human head, which rises out of the four elements of the body. This sacred mountain, upon whose summit stood the temple of the gods, gave rise to the stories of Olympus, Meru, and Asgard. The City of the Golden Gates--the capital of Atlantis--is the one now preserved among numerous religions as the *City of the Gods* or the *Holy City*. Here is the archetype of the New Jerusalem, with its streets paved with gold and its twelve gates shining with precious stones.

"The history of Atlantis," writes Ignatius Donnelly, "is the key of the Greek mythology. There can be no question that these gods of Greece were human beings. The tendency to attach divine attributes to great earthly rulers is one deeply implanted in human nature."[5]

The same author sustains his views by noting that the deities of the Greek pantheon were not looked upon as creators of the universe but rather as regents set over it by its more ancient original fabricators. The Garden of Eden from which humanity was driven by a flaming sword is perhaps an allusion to the earthly paradise supposedly located west of the Pillars of

---

[5] See *Atlantis*

Hercules and destroyed by volcanic cataclysms. The Deluge legend may be traced also to the Atlantean inundation, during which a "world" was destroyed by water.

Was the religious, philosophic, and scientific knowledge possessed by the priestcrafts of antiquity secured from Atlantis, whose submergence obliterated every vestige of its part in the drama of world progress? Atlantean sun worship has been perpetuated in the ritualism and ceremonialism of both Christianity and pagandom. Both the cross and the serpent were Atlantean emblems of divine wisdom. The divine[6] progenitors of the Mayas and Quichés of Central America coexisted within the green and azure radiance of Gucumatz, the "plumed" serpent. The six sky-born sages came into manifestation as centers of light bound together or synthesized by the seventh--and chief--of their order, the "feathered" snake.[7] The title of "winged" or "plumed" snake was applied to Quetzalcoatl, or Kukulcan, the Central American initiate. The center of the Atlantean Wisdom-Religion was presumably a great pyramidal temple standing on the brow of a plateau rising in the midst of the City of the Golden Gates. From here the Initiate-Priests of the Sacred Feather went forth, carrying the keys of Universal Wisdom to the uttermost parts of the earth.

The mythologies of many nations contain accounts of gods who "came out of the sea." Certain *shamans* among the American Indians tell of holy men dressed in birds' feathers and wampum who rose out of the blue waters and instructed them

---

[6] Atlantean
[7] See the *Popol Vuh*

in the arts and crafts. Among the legends of the Chaldeans is that of Oannes, a partly amphibious creature who came out of the sea and taught the savage peoples along the shore to read and write, till the soil, cultivate herbs for healing, study the stars, establish rational forms of government, and become conversant with the sacred Mysteries. Among the Mayas, Quetzalcoatl, the Savior-God,[8] issued from the waters and, after instructing the people in the essentials of civilization, rode out to sea on a magic raft of serpents to escape the wrath of the fierce god of the Fiery Mirror, Tezcatlipoca.

May it not have been that these demigods of a fabulous age who, Esdras-like, came out of the sea were Atlantean priests? All that primitive man remembered of the Atlanteans was the glory of their golden ornaments, the transcendency of their wisdom, and the sanctity of their symbols--the cross and the serpent. That they came in ships was soon forgotten, for untutored minds considered even boats as supernatural. Wherever the Atlanteans proselyted they erected pyramids and temples patterned after the great sanctuary in the City of the Golden Gates. Such is the origin of the pyramids of Egypt, Mexico, and Central America. The mounds in Normandy and Britain, as well as those of the American Indians, are remnants of a similar culture. In the midst of the Atlantean program of world colonization and conversion, the cataclysms which sank Atlantis began. The Initiate-Priests of the Sacred Feather who promised to come back to their missionary settlements never returned; and after the lapse of centuries tradition preserved

---

[8] whom some Christian scholars believe to have been St. Thomas

only a fantastic account of gods who came from a place where the sea now is.

H. P. Blavatsky[9] thus sums up the causes which precipitated the Atlantean disaster: "Under the evil insinuations of their demon, Thevetat, the Atlantis-race became a nation of wicked *magicians*. In consequence of this, war was declared, the story of which would be too long to narrate; its substance may be found in the disfigured allegories of the race of Cain, the giants, and that of Noah and his righteous family. The conflict came to an end by the submersion of the Atlantis; which finds its imitation in the stories of the Babylonian and Mosaic flood: The giants and magicians '...and all flesh died...and every man.' All except Xisuthrus and Noah, who are substantially identical with the great Father of the Thlinkithians in the *Popol Vuh*,[10] or the sacred book of the Guatemaleans, which also tells of his escaping in a large boat, like the Hindu Noah-- Vaiswasvata."[11]

From the Atlanteans the world has received not only the heritage of arts and crafts, philosophies and sciences, ethics and

---

[9] Madame Helena Petrovna Blavatsky was a Russian philosopher and author who co-founded the Theosophical Society in 1875. She gained an international following as the leading theoretician of Theosophy.

[10] The *Popol Vuh* is a foundational sacred narrative of the K'iche' people from long before the Spanish conquest of Mexico. It includes the Mayan creation myth, the exploits of the Hero Twins Hunahpú and Xbalanqué, and a chronicle of the K'iche' people. The name "Popol Vuh" translates as "Book of the People". It was originally preserved through oral tradition until approximately 1550, when it was recorded in writing. The documentation of the *Popol Vuh* is credited to the 18th-century Spanish Dominican friar Francisco Ximénez, who prepared a manuscript with a transcription in K'iche' and parallel columns with translations into Spanish.

[11] See *Isis Unveiled*

religions, but also the heritage of hate, strife, and perversion. The Atlanteans instigated the first war; and it has been said that all subsequent wars were fought in a fruitless effort to justify the first one and right the wrong which it caused. Before Atlantis sank, its spiritually illumined Initiates, who realized that their land was doomed because it had departed from the Path of Light, withdrew from the ill-fated continent. Carrying with them the sacred and secret doctrine, these Atlanteans established themselves in Egypt, where they became its first "divine" rulers. Nearly all the great cosmologic myths forming the foundation of the various sacred books of the world are based upon the Atlantean Mystery rituals.

Part II:
The Myth of the Dying God

The myth of *Tammuz* and *Ishtar* is one of the earliest examples of the dying-god allegory, probably antedating 4000 B. C.[12] The imperfect condition of the tablets upon which the legends are inscribed makes it impossible to secure more than a fragmentary account of the Tammuz rites. Being the esoteric god of the sun, Tammuz did not occupy a position among the first deities venerated by the Babylonians, who for lack of deeper knowledge looked upon him as a god of agriculture or a vegetation spirit. Originally he was described as being one of the guardians of the gates of the underworld. Like many other Savior-Gods, he is referred to as a "shepherd" or "the lord of the shepherd seat." Tammuz occupies the remarkable position of son and husband of Ishtar, the Babylonian and Assyrian Mother-goddess. Ishtar--to whom the planet Venus was sacred--was the most widely venerated deity of the Babylonian and Assyrian pantheon. She was probably identical with Ashteroth, Astarte, and Aphrodite. The story of her descent into the underworld in search presumably for the sacred elixir which alone could restore Tammuz to life is the key to the ritual of her Mysteries. Tammuz, whose annual festival took place just before the summer solstice, died in midsummer in the ancient month which bore his name, and was mourned with elaborate ceremonies. The manner of his death is unknown, but some of the accusations made against Ishtar by Izdubar[13] would

---

[12] See *Babylonia and Assyria* by Lewis Spence
[13] Nimrod

indicate that she, indirectly at least, had contributed to his demise. The resurrection of Tammuz was the occasion of great rejoicing, at which time he was hailed as a "redeemer" of his people.

With outspread wings, Ishtar, the daughter of Sin,[14] sweeps downward to the gates of death. The house of darkness--the dwelling of the god Irkalla--is described as "the place of no return." It is without light; the nourishment of those who dwell therein is dust and their food is mud. Over the bolts on the door of the house of Irkalla is scattered dust, and the keepers of the house are covered with feathers like birds. Ishtar demands that the keepers open the gates, declaring that if they do not she will shatter the doorposts and strike the hinges and raise up dead devourers of the living. The guardians of the gates beg her to be patient while they go to the queen of Hades from whom they secure permission to admit Ishtar, but only in the same manner as all others came to this dreary house. Ishtar thereupon descends through the seven gates which lead downward into the depths of the underworld. At the first gate the great crown is removed from her head, at the second gate the earrings from her ears, at the third gate the necklace from her neck, at the fourth gate the ornaments from her breast, at the fifth gate the girdle from her waist, at the sixth gate the bracelets from her hands and feet, and at the seventh gate the covering cloak of her body. Ishtar remonstrates as each successive article of apparel is taken from her, but the guardian tells her that this is the experience of all who enter the somber domain of death. Enraged upon beholding Ishtar, the Mistress

---

[14] the Moon

of Hades inflicts upon her all manner of disease and imprisons her in the underworld.

As Ishtar represents the spirit of fertility, her loss prevents the ripening of the crops and the maturing of all life upon the earth.

In this respect the story parallels the legend of Persephone. The gods, realizing that the loss of Ishtar is disorganizing all Nature, send a messenger to the underworld and demand her release. The Mistress of Hades is forced to comply, and the water of life is poured over Ishtar. Thus cured of the infirmities inflicted on her, she retraces her way upward through the seven gates, at each of which she is reinvested with the article of apparel which the guardians had removed.[15] No record exists that Ishtar secured the water of life which would have wrought the resurrection of Tammuz.

The myth of Ishtar symbolizes the descent of the human spirit through the seven worlds, or spheres of the sacred planets, until finally, deprived of its spiritual adornments, it incarnates in the physical body--Hades--where the mistress of that body heaps every form of sorrow and misery upon the imprisoned consciousness. The waters of life--the secret doctrine--cure the diseases of ignorance; and the spirit, ascending again to its divine source, regains its God-given adornments as it passes upward through the rings of the planets.

---

[15] See *The Chaldean Account of Genesis*

Another Mystery ritual among the Babylonians and Assyrians was that of Merodach and the Dragon. Merodach, the creator of the inferior universe, slays a horrible monster and out of her body forms the universe. Here is the probable source of the so-called Christian allegory of St. George and the Dragon.

The Mysteries of *Adonis*, or *Adoni*, were celebrated annually in many parts of Egypt, Phœnicia, and Biblos. The name *Adonis*, or *Adoni*, means "Lord" and was a designation applied to the sun and later borrowed by the Jews as the exoteric name of their God. Smyrna, mother of Adonis, was turned into a tree by the gods and after a time the bark burst open and the infant Savior issued forth. According to one account, he was liberated by a wild boar which split the wood of the maternal tree with its tusks. Adonis was born at midnight of the 24th of December, and through his unhappy death a Mystery rite was established that wrought the salvation of his people. In the Jewish month of Tammuz[16] he was gored to death by a wild boar sent by the god Ars.[17] The *Adoniasmos* was the ceremony of lamenting the premature death of the murdered god.

In Ezekiel viii. 14[18], it is written that women were weeping for Tammuz[19] at the north gate of the Lord's House in Jerusalem. Sir James George Frazer cites Jerome thus: "He tells

---

[16] another name for this deity

[17] Mars

[18] *Then he brought me to the door of the gate of the Lord's house which was toward the north; and, behold, there sat women weeping for Tammuz.*

[19] Adonis

us that Bethlehem, the traditionary birthplace of the Lord, was shaded by a grove of that still older Syrian Lord, Adonis, and that where the infant Jesus had wept, the lover of Venus was bewailed."[20] The effigy of a wild boar is said to have been set over one of the gates of Jerusalem in honor of Adonis, and his rites celebrated in the grotto of the Nativity at Bethlehem. Adonis as the "gored"[21] man is one of the keys to Sir Francis Bacon's use of the "wild boar" in his cryptic symbolism.

Adonis was originally an androgynous deity who represented the solar power which in the winter was destroyed by the evil principle of cold--the boar. After three days[22] in the tomb, Adonis rose triumphant on the 25th day of March, amidst the acclamation of his priests and followers, "He is risen!" Adonis was born out of a myrrh tree. Myrrh, the symbol of death because of its connection with the process of embalming, was one of the gifts brought by the three Magi to the manger of Jesus.

In the Mysteries of Adonis the neophyte passed through the symbolic death of the god and, "raised" by the priests, entered into the blessed state of redemption made possible by the sufferings of Adonis. Nearly all authors believe Adonis to have been originally a vegetation god directly connected with the growth and maturing of flowers and fruits. In support of this viewpoint they describe the "gardens of Adonis, " which were small baskets of earth in which seeds were planted and

---

[20] See *The Golden Bough.*
[21] or "god"
[22] months

nurtured for a period of eight days. When those plants prematurely died for lack of sufficient earth, they were considered emblematic of the murdered Adonis and were usually cast into the sea with images of the god.

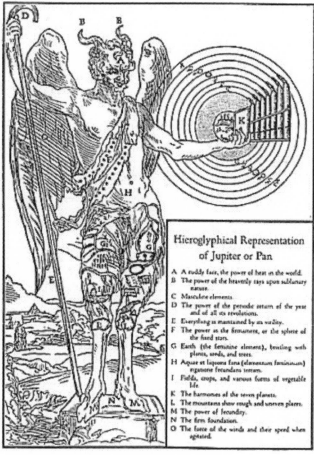

THE GREAT GOD PAN. From Kircher's *Œdipus Ægyptiacus*.[23]

---

[23] The great Pan was celebrated as the author and director of the sacred dances which he is supposed to have instituted to symbolize the circumambulations of the heavenly bodies. Pan was a composite creature, the upper part--with the exception of his horns--being human, and the lower part in the form of a goat. Pan is the prototype of natural energy and, while undoubtedly a phallic deity, should nor be confused with Priapus. The pipes of Pan signify the natural harmony of the spheres, and the god himself is a symbol of Saturn because this planet is enthroned in Capricorn, whose emblem is a

In Phrygia there existed a remarkable school of religious philosophy which centered around the life and untimely fate of another Savior-God known as *Atys*, or *Attis*, by many considered synonymous with Adonis. This deity was born at midnight on the 24th day of December. Of his death there are two accounts. In one he was gored to death like Adonis; in the other he emasculated himself under a pine tree and there died. His body was taken to a cave by the Great Mother,[24] where it remained through the ages without decaying. To the rites of Atys the modern world is indebted for the symbolism of the Christmas tree. Atys imparted his immortality to the tree beneath which he died, and Cybele took the tree with her when she removed the body. Atys remained three days in the tomb, rose upon a date corresponding with Easter morn, and by this resurrection overcame death for all who were initiated into his Mysteries.

"In the Mysteries of the Phrygians," says Julius Firmicus, "which are called those of the MOTHER OF THE GODS, every year a PINE TREE is cut down and in the inside of the tree the image of a YOUTH is tied in! In the Mysteries of Isis the trunk of a PINE TREE is cut: the middle of the trunk is nicely hollowed out; the idol of Osiris made from those hollowed pieces is BURIED. In the Mysteries of Proserpine a tree cut is put together into the effigy and form of the VIRGIN,

---

goat. The Egyptians were initiated into the Mysteries of Pan, who was regarded as a phase of Jupiter, the Demiurgus. Pan represented the impregnating power of the sun and was the chief of a horde rustic deities, and satyrs. He also signified the controlling spirit of the lower worlds. The fabricated a story to the effect that at the time of the birth of Christ the oracles were silenced after giving utterance to one last cry, "Great Pan is dead!"

[24] Cybele

and when it has been carried within the city it is MOURNED 40 nights, but the fortieth night it is BURNED!"[25]

The Mysteries of Atys included a sacramental meal during which the neophyte ate out of a drum and drank from a cymbal. After being baptized by the blood of a bull, the new initiate was fed entirely on milk to symbolize that he was still a philosophical infant, having but recently been born out of the sphere of materiality.[26] Is there a possible connection between this lacteal diet prescribed by the Attic rite and St. Paul's allusion to the food for spiritual babes? Sallust gives a key to the esoteric interpretation of the Attic rituals. Cybele, the Great Mother, signifies the vivifying powers of the universe, and Atys that aspect of the spiritual intellect which is suspended between the divine and animal spheres. The Mother of the gods, loving Atys, gave him a starry hat, signifying celestial powers, but Atys,[27] falling in love with a nymph,[28] forfeited his divinity and lost his creative powers. It is thus evident that Atys represents the human consciousness and that his Mysteries are concerned with the reattainment of the starry hat.[29]

The rites of *Sabazius* were very similar to those of Bacchus and it is generally believed that the two deities are identical. Bacchus was born at Sabazius, or Sabaoth, and these names are frequently assigned to him. The Sabazian Mysteries were performed at night, and the ritual included the drawing of a live

---

[25] See Sod, *the Mysteries of Adoni.*
[26] See Frazer's *The Golden Bough.*
[27] mankind
[28] symbolic of the lower animal propensities
[29] See *Sallust on the Gods and the World.*

snake across the breast of the candidate. Clement of Alexandria writes: "The token of the Sabazian Mysteries to the initiated is 'the deity gliding over the breast.'" A golden serpent was the symbol of Sabazius because this deity represented the annual renovation of the world by the solar power. The Jews borrowed the name Sabaoth from these Mysteries and adopted it as one of the appellations of their supreme God. During the time the Sabazian Mysteries were celebrated in Rome, the cult gained many votaries and later influenced the symbolism of Christianity.

The Cabiric Mysteries of Samothrace were renowned among the ancients, being next to the Eleusinian in public esteem. Herodotus declares that the Samothracians received their doctrines, especially those concerning Mercury, from the Pelasgians. Little is known concerning the Cabiric rituals, for they were enshrouded in the profoundest secrecy. Some regard the Cabiri as seven in number and refer to them as "the Seven Spirits of fire before the throne of Saturn." Others believe the Cabiri to be the seven sacred wanderers, later called the planets.

While a vast number of deities are associated with the Samothracian Mysteries, the ritualistic drama centers around four brothers. The first three--Aschieros, Achiochersus, and Achiochersa--attack and murder the fourth—Cashmala.[30] Dionysidorus, however, identifies Aschieros with Demeter, Achiochersus with Pluto, Achiochersa with Persephone, and Cashmala with Hermes. Alexander Wilder notes that in the Samothracian ritual "Cadmillus is made to include the Theban

---

[30] or Cadmillus

Serpent-god, Cadmus, the Thoth of Egypt, the Hermes of the Greeks, and the Emeph or Æsculapius of the Alexandrians and Phœnicians." Here again is a repetition of the story of Osiris, Bacchus, Adonis, Balder, and Hiram Abiff.[31] The worship of Atys and Cybele was also involved in the Samothracian Mysteries. In the rituals of the Cabiri is to be traced a form of pine-tree worship, for this tree, sacred to Atys, was first trimmed into the form of a cross and then cut down in honor of the murdered god whose body was discovered at its foot.

"If you wish to inspect the orgies of the Corybantes," writes Clement, "Then know that, having killed their third brother, they covered the head of the dead body with a purple cloth, crowned it, and carrying it on the point of a spear, buried it under the roots of Olympus. These mysteries are, in short, murders and funerals.[32] And the priests Of these rites, who are called kings of the sacred rites by those whose business it is to name them, give additional strangeness to the tragic occurrence, by forbidding parsley with the roots from being placed on the table, for they think that parsley grew from the Corybantic blood that flowed forth; just as the women, in celebrating the Thcsmophoria, abstain from eating the seeds of the pomegranate, which have fallen on the ground, from the

---

[31] Hiram Abiff (*the Widow's son*) is the central character of an allegory presented to all candidates during the third degree in Freemasonry, in which the candidate represents the Widow's son. Hiram is presented as the chief architect of King Solomon's Temple. He is murdered inside this Temple by three ruffians, after they failed to obtain from him the Master Masons' secret passwords. The themes of the allegory are the importance of fidelity, and the certainty of death.

[32] This ante-Nicene Father in his efforts to defame the pagan rites apparently ignores the fact that, like the Cabirian martyr, Jesus Christ was foully betrayed, tortured, and finally murdered!

idea that pomegranates sprang from the drops of the blood of Dionysus. Those Corybantes also they call Cabiric; and the ceremony itself they announce as the Cabiric mystery."

The Mysteries of the Cabiri were divided into three degrees, the first of which celebrated the death of Cashmala, at the hands of his three brothers; the second, the discovery of his mutilated body, the parts of which had been found and gathered after much labor; and the third--accompanied by great rejoicing and happiness--his resurrection and the consequent salvation of the world. The temple of the Cabiri at Samothrace contained a number of curious divinities, many of them misshapen creatures representing the elemental powers of Nature, possibly the Bacchic Titans. Children were initiated into the Cabirian cult with the same dignity as adults, and criminals who reached the sanctuary were safe from pursuit. The Samothracian rites were particularly concerned with navigation, the Dioscuri--Castor and Pollux, or the gods of navigation--being among those propitiated by members of that cult. The Argonautic expedition, listening to the advice of Orpheus, stopped at the island of Samothrace for the purpose of having its members initiated into the Cabiric rites.

Herodotus relates that when Cambyses entered the temple of the Cabiri he was unable to restrain his mirth at seeing before him the figure of a man standing upright and, facing the man, the figure of a woman standing on her head. Had Cambyses been acquainted with the principles of divine astronomy, he would have realized that he was then in the presence of the key to universal equilibrium. "'I ask,' says Voltaire, 'who were these

Hierophants, these sacred Freemasons, who celebrated their Ancient Mysteries of Samothracia, and whence came they and their gods Cabiri?'"[33] Clement speaks of the Mysteries of the Cabiri as "the sacred Mystery of a brother slain by his brethren," and the "Cabiric death" was one of the secret symbols of antiquity. Thus the allegory of the Self murdered by the not-self is perpetuated through the religious mysticism of all peoples. The *philosophic death* and the *philosophic resurrection* are the Lesser and the Greater Mysteries respectively.

A curious aspect of the *dying-god* myth is that of the Hanged Man. The most important example of this peculiar conception is found in the Odinic rituals where Odin hangs himself for nine nights from the branches of the World Tree and upon the same occasion also pierces his own side with the sacred spear. As the result of this great sacrifice, Odin, while suspended over the depths of Nifl-heim, discovered by meditation the runes or alphabets by which later the records of his people were preserved. Because of this remarkable experience, Odin is sometimes shown seated on a gallows tree and he became the patron deity of all who died by the noose. Esoterically, the Hanged Man is the human spirit which is suspended from heaven by a single thread. Wisdom, not death, is the reward for this voluntary sacrifice during which the human soul, suspended above the world of illusion, and meditating upon its unreality, is rewarded by the achievement of self-realization.

From a consideration of all these ancient and secret rituals it becomes evident that the mystery of the *dying god* was

---

[33] See Mackey's *Encyclopædia of Freemasonry.*

universal among the illumined and venerated colleges of the sacred teaching. This mystery has been perpetuated in Christianity in the crucifixion and death of the God-man-Jesus the Christ. The secret import of this world tragedy and the Universal Martyr must be rediscovered if Christianity is to reach the heights attained by the pagans in the days of their philosophic supremacy. The myth of the dying god is the key to both universal and individual redemption and regeneration, and those who do not comprehend the true nature of this supreme allegory are not privileged to consider themselves either wise or truly religious.

Made in the USA
Monee, IL
03 January 2023

24087973R00021